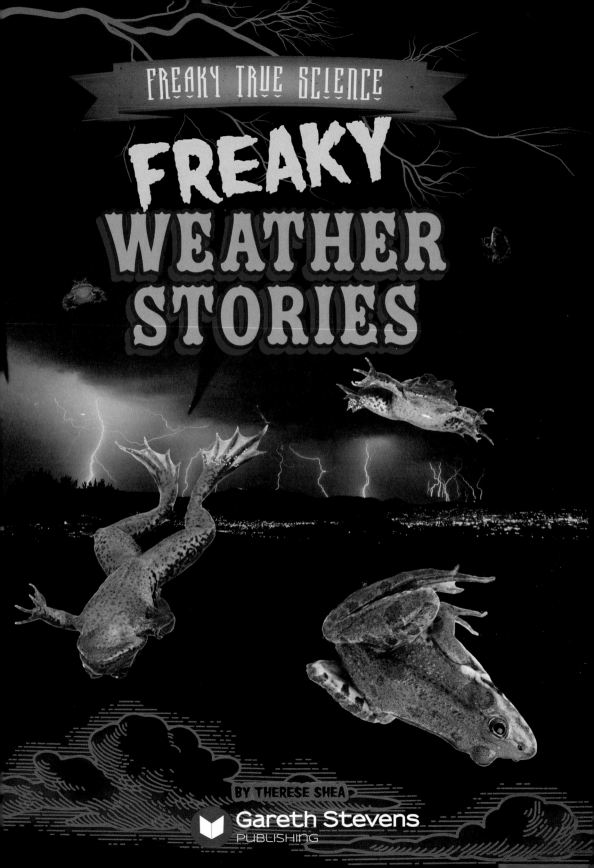

FREAKY TRUE SCIENCE

FREAKY WEATHER STORIES

BY THERESE SHEA

Gareth Stevens
PUBLISHING

Please visit our website, www.garethstevens.com. For a free color catalog of all our high-quality books, call toll free 1-800-542-2595 or fax 1-877-542-2596.

Cataloging-in-Publication Data

Shea, Therese.
Freaky weather stories / by Therese Shea.
p. cm. — (Freaky true science)
Includes index.
ISBN 978-1-4824-2968-8 (pbk.)
ISBN 978-1-4824-2969-5 (6 pack)
ISBN 978-1-4824-2970-1 (library binding)
1. Weather — Miscellanea — Juvenile literature. 2. Meteorology — Miscellanea — Juvenile literature. I. Shea, Therese. II. Title.
QC981.3 S54 2016
551.6—d23

First Edition

Published in 2016 by
Gareth Stevens Publishing
111 East 14th Street, Suite 349
New York, NY 10003

Copyright © 2016 Gareth Stevens Publishing

Designer: Sarah Liddell
Editor: Ryan Nagelhout

Photo credits: Cover, p. 1 (lightning bolt) Potapov Alexander/Shutterstock.com; cover, p. 1 (cloud used throughout book) Mila Petkova/Shutterstock.com; cover, p. 1 (storm) swa182/Shutterstock.com; cover, p. 1 (frog upper right and lower right) USBFCO/Shutterstock.com; cover, p. 1 (frog upper left) Smit/Shutterstock.com; cover, p. 1 (frog middle and lower left) JDCarballo/Shutterstock.com; background throughout book leedsn/Shutterstock.com; pp. 5, 7, 9, 11, 13, 15, 17, 19, 21, 23, 25, 27, 29 (hand used throughout) Helena Ohman/Shutterstock.com; pp. 5, 7, 9, 11, 13, 15, 17, 19, 21, 23, 25, 27, 29 (texture throughout) Alex Gontar/Shutterstock.com; p. 5 Simon Laprida/Shutterstock.com; p. 7 photo courtesy of NOAA; p. 9 Joe Thomissen/Wikimedia Commons; p. 10 Anadolu Agency/Contributor/Anadolu Agency/Getty Images; p. 11 NordicPhotos/Contributor/Getty Images News/Getty Images; p. 13 Jessica McGowan/Stringer/Getty Images News/Getty Images; p. 14 AlbertHerring/Wikimedia Commons; p. 15 Dolovis/Wikimedia Commons; p. 17 Minerva Studio/Shutterstock.com; p. 19 (roll cloud) Danielaeberl/Wikimedia Commons; p. 19 (shelf cloud) Dub/Wikimedia Commons; p. 21 Print Collector/Contributor/Hulton Archive/Getty Images; p. 22 (under microscope) Melesse/Wikimedia Commons; p. 22 (rain sample) Grook Da Oger/Wikimedia Commons; p. 23 B.navez/Wikimedia Commons; p. 25 Saibo/Wikimedia Commons; p. 27 JialiangGao/Wikimedia Commons; p. 29 (upside-down rainbow) Thiebes/Wikimedia Commons; p. 29 (snow roll) Salvi 5/Wikimedia Commons; p. 29 (aurora) Quibik/Wikimedia Commons; p. 29 (red sprite) Saperaud~commonswiki/Wikimedia Commons; p. 29 (mammatus clouds) Bizenya/Wikimedia Commons; p. 29 (microburst) photo courtesy of NOAA Legacy Photo ERL/WPL.

Printed in the United States of America

CONTENTS

Words in the glossary appear in **bold** type
the first time they are used in the text.

FREAKY FORECASTS

Weather can be really freaky, which means it can be unusual, strange, or bizarre. If weather were easy to figure out, then the weather forecast would always be right. It often isn't! Even with all the scientific equipment of today, temperatures can be much hotter or colder than predicted, or forecast. Winds kick up, storms form, and rain and snow fall when they're not expected to. Sometimes even predicted weather seems freaky. Blizzards, hurricanes, and tornadoes can be some of the most terrifying weather events, causing incredible amounts of destruction and even threatening lives.

In this book, you'll learn about some of the freakiest weather ever to occur on Earth. Some **phenomena** are just plain weird. And some are so bizarre that scientists can't even explain them!

FREAKY FACTS!

During ancient times, freaky or bad weather was often blamed on gods or spirits.

WHAT IS WEATHER?

Weather is the state of the atmosphere. It includes temperature, cloudiness, **precipitation**, wind, **humidity**, and air pressure. Earth's weather takes place in the troposphere, which is the lowest region of the atmosphere that extends from the planet's surface up to 4 to 5 miles (6 to 8 km) above it at the North and South Poles and to about 10 miles (16 km) above the surface at the equator. Weather affects many parts of human life, from where we live to what we eat.

WEATHER SHOULDN'T BE CONFUSED WITH CLIMATE, WHICH IS THE AVERAGE WEATHER OF A PLACE OVER MANY YEARS. WEATHER IS WHAT'S HAPPENING NOW IN THE LOWER ATMOSPHERE.

HORRIBLE HAIL

Usually, stormy days are a pain in some ways. They mean people can't do normal outdoor activities. However, some storms mean real pain—painful precipitation! Hail is rain that has been lifted high into the atmosphere and frozen. It comes back down as pieces of ice. Large hailstones can especially hurt. Hail becomes larger the more it's tossed around in the atmosphere. The hailstone grows layer by layer.

You can probably imagine how painful it would be to be hit by a fastball during a baseball game. Some hailstones fall at a rate of 100 miles (161 km) per hour. That speed is the reason why hailstorms can cause a lot of damage, such as breaking windows, destroying crops, and putting dents and even holes in roofs.

FREAKY FACTS!

Hail can kill livestock and people.

HOW BIG?

The largest hailstone recorded in the United States so far was
18 inches (46 cm) around and weighed 2 pounds (907 g). And it was
measured after melting a bit! This piece of ice was found on the
property of a Vivian, South Dakota, resident after a particularly
violent thunderstorm. Even small hailstones can cause great damage,
though. It's thought hail is the cause of almost $1 billion in damage
to property and crops each year in the United States alone.

STRANGE LIGHTNING

Lightning is pretty freaky. It's electricity in the air! Lightning occurs when particles within clouds build up too much of a positive or negative electric charge. The buildup seeks an area in which there's a buildup of the opposite electric charge. When the opposite charges meet, they create an electric current called lightning. During a thunderstorm, lightning can occur within a cloud, between clouds, between a cloud and the air, or between a cloud and the ground.

There's one kind of lightning that's so rare many scientists didn't even believe it existed for a long time. It's called ball lightning, and it looks like its name. Ball lightning can be as large as a beach ball and have a yellow, orange, or blue color. It smokes as it travels slowly through the air until it disappears.

FREAKY FACTS!

Lightning kills about 50 people each year in the United States, according to the National Weather Service.

STUDYING SILICON

Scientists needed to see ball lightning for themselves to believe it! One scientist saw it in an airplane before studying it seriously. It floated through the plane's walls! Though there are still many questions about ball lightning, one study shows that the dust of the element silicon binds together in the air into a ball when struck by lightning. The ball heats and glows until the silicon burns out. Ball lightning has even been made in a lab!

BALL LIGHTNING CAN BE JUST AS DANGEROUS AS OTHER KINDS OF LIGHTNING, SETTING FIRES AND INJURING PEOPLE.

There's another surprising place to spot lightning—a volcanic eruption! Large eruptions especially create spectacular lightning strikes. Smaller eruptions might create lightning, too, but it's harder to see among the ash clouds that emerge from the volcano.

So how do volcanoes make lightning? Scientists think the matter that comes out of the volcano and enters the atmosphere is positively charged. Because of this, areas of negative charges begin to form in a cloud. A lightning bolt eventually travels through the air to connect these areas to balance out the charges. It's thought there may be different types of lightning occurring around the volcano, too. One kind happens just around the mouth, while another kind takes place in the highest ranges of the **plume**.

FREAKY FACTS!

Volcanic lightning is sometimes found as far as 90 miles (145 km) from the volcano!

ELECTRIC ERUPTION

Scientists aren't sure why volcanic matter is positively charged and if it's like this within the volcano or just when it erupts. A recent study suggests that ash becomes charged as magma breaks up within the volcano. However, we know that volcanoes cause lightning farther away from the mouth, too. These lightning bolts may form similarly to the lightning in thunderstorms. Scientist Sonja Behnke studied plumes as large as 11 miles (18 km) wide and found they generated thousands of lightning bolts.

TORNADO TERROR

Imagine watching a thunderstorm from inside your house and suddenly seeing a vertical column of rotating air reach down from the clouds—a tornado! Tornadoes are definitely freaky. It's not that they're rare; far from it. About 1,200 tornadoes are thought to hit the United States each year. Most are so weak or small that they're not even noticed or reported. However, some are so strong their winds reach speeds over 300 miles (483 km) per hour.

One tornado is bad enough. What about more than 300 hitting the same area? From April 25 through April 28, 2011, about 350 tornadoes tore across the eastern United States, with the worst touching down in Mississippi, Alabama, Tennessee, and Georgia. **Meteorologists** called this occurrence a "Super Outbreak." Sadly, 321 people were killed.

FREAKY FACTS!

In the Northern Hemisphere, tornadoes usually rotate in a counterclockwise direction. In the Southern Hemisphere, tornadoes usually rotate in a clockwise direction.

NOW YOU SEE IT . . .

Some tornadoes seem to appear out of nowhere and then disappear just as quickly as they came. While in action, tornadoes uproot trees, power lines, and buildings and threaten people's lives. Unfortunately, it's very hard to predict when a thunderstorm will produce a tornado. Currently, the warning time for a tornado is just 13 minutes. This is short, but can be enough time to run to a safe place, such as a storm shelter or a basement.

MOST OF THE 2011 SUPER OUTBREAK TORNADOES OCCURRED ON APRIL 27. ONE OF THE HARDEST-HIT AREAS WAS TUSCALOOSA, ALABAMA, WHERE A TORNADO WITH A **DIAMETER** OF NEARLY 1 MILE (1.6 KM) CAUSED TERRIBLE DESTRUCTION.

Tornadoes definitely are scary weather phenomena. Their powerful spinning winds can rip trees, cars, and even buildings from the ground. But can you picture those winds spinning with fire? That's not a creation of someone's imagination: that's real weather!

They're called fire tornadoes, fire whirls, or firenadoes, and they can occur during a fire. A sudden change in wind speed and direction causes rising hot air to begin to spin and lift into a vertical column. Cool air rushes in to take the place of the hot air, heats up in the burning conditions, and continues the firenado. Just like tornadoes pick up and throw debris, firenadoes throw **embers** and sparks, helping spread an existing fire as it travels.

FREAKY FACTS!

Firenadoes can be as wide as 500 feet (152 m)!

FIRE WHIRL

REALLY WILD FIRE

The 2014 wildfires in San Diego County, California, produced multiple fire tornadoes, making a risky situation even more dangerous for firefighters to control. Firenadoes don't just happen in natural settings, though. The Great Chicago Fire of 1871 produced a firenado that tossed pieces of burning wood at other parts of the city, enabling the fire to spread quickly. Scientists think firenadoes burn fuel up to seven times faster than a normal fire.

Tornadoes develop over all kinds of landforms—and even water! Tornadoes that form over water or that move from land to water are called waterspouts. There are two kinds: tornadic waterspouts, which touch down from thunderstorms, and fair-weather waterspouts, which form from the water upward. Fair-weather waterspouts are more common than tornadic and are less dangerous. However, both types can threaten swimmers, boaters, and aircraft.

The largest waterspouts can be 330 feet (100 m) wide, last up to 1 hour, and have winds around 190 miles (306 km) per hour. However, the average waterspout's lifetime is just 5 to 10 minutes. Scientists have flown into waterspouts to study them. One scientist, Joseph Golden, reported that even a weak waterspout's winds "rattled" his teeth.

FREAKY FACTS!

Waterspouts usually require warm water. However, there have been reports of snowspouts forming over cold waters in winter!

BERMUDA TRIANGLE

The Bermuda Triangle is an area between Miami, Florida; the island of Bermuda; and Puerto Rico where many ships and airplanes have disappeared mysteriously. This region, with its warm, tropical waters, is known for frequent waterspouts. In fact, the area around the Florida Keys is the "waterspout capital of the world." Waterspouts may explain some strange occurrences that have happened in the Bermuda Triangle. A strong waterspout could suck a plane out of the sky or damage a boat.

TORNADIC WATERSPOUTS MAY BE ACCOMPANIED BY LIGHTNING AND HAIL, MAKING THEM EVEN MORE DANGEROUS.

CRAZY CLOUDS

If you needed proof that Earth's atmosphere is a freaky place, just look to the clouds. A roll cloud is a low, **horizontal** cloud that's shaped like a tube. It's not attached to any other cloud. This rare formation can look like a tornado funnel that's been turned on its side. Two important differences are that a roll cloud doesn't touch the ground like a tornado funnel does and it doesn't rotate vertically.

Shelf clouds are low, horizontal clouds with a curved shape. Unlike roll clouds, they're attached to a "parent" cloud. They stick out like a shelf or plow. Both shelf clouds and roll clouds are a result of downdrafts, or air currents pushing cold air down and making warm, moist air rise to **condense** into clouds.

FREAKY FACTS!

Sometimes, rain and hail may come out of a cloud in the shape of a column. These, too, can look like tornadoes.

CLOUD WATCH

Shelf clouds often develop at the front of a thunderstorm. Sometimes shelf clouds look like the clouds from which tornadoes can form—mesocyclones—but you can easily spot the difference. Shelf clouds don't rotate vertically like mesocyclones do. Instead, the upper part of the cloud looks like it's rising. If you do see a massive cloud rotating vertically, check the weather report and be ready to get to a safe place—a tornado may be on its way!

SHELF CLOUD

ROLL CLOUD

ARCUS CLOUDS ARE LOW, HORIZONTAL CLOUD FORMATIONS. ROLL CLOUDS AND SHELF CLOUDS ARE TWO KINDS OF ARCUS CLOUDS.

19

IT'S RAINING WHAT?

Did you ever hear the saying "it's raining cats and dogs"? That means it's raining a lot. Sometimes, stranger things than water come out of the clouds, though! Waterspouts have been known to suck fish and other creatures out of oceans and lakes and drop them over land.

That's what happened in May 2014 in western Sri Lanka. Villagers heard objects falling heavily on their roofs and roads and saw a mass of fish lying on the ground outside. Some people collected the fish in buckets, so they could eat them later! Another part of Sri Lanka had a similar "animal shower" in 2012. That year, many prawns, which are small creatures somewhat like shrimp, fell from the sky.

FREAKY FACTS!

Reports say tadpoles have fallen over Japan, spiders over Brazil, frogs over Serbia and Egypt, snails over England, eels over Alabama, and snakes over Tennessee!

"ANIMAL RAIN" IS SO RARE THAT IT'S HARD TO FIND PHOTOS OF THE PHENOMENON. HOWEVER, PEOPLE THROUGHOUT HISTORY HAVE DRAWN PICTURES AND CREATED PAINTINGS OF THE UNUSUAL OCCURRENCE.

WEIRD WEATHER

Sometimes, the animals that come down from a tornado or waterspout are still alive, as they were in Sri Lanka in 2014. Other times, if they're lifted high into the atmosphere, they freeze. Violent tornado winds may also tear animals apart so just tiny body parts rain down. Yuck! There have even been reports of animals raining down when there's no rain! In that case, strong winds must somehow carry the creatures very long distances.

21

Rainstorms aren't that freaky. However, we're used to rain coming down in clear drops of water. Can you imagine a red rain? That's what happened in southwestern India in 2001 over a period of 2 months. It wasn't the first time it had occurred, either. There are records from as far back as AD 582 of red rain—or "blood rain" as it's sometimes called—pouring down on the people of Paris, France. But the 2001 rain in India was finally able to be collected and examined by modern scientists.

A study by the Indian government found that the rain contained solid particles that gave it its color. They believe the red particles are **spores** from algae. These algae form **lichen** that has been found in the region.

FREAKY FACTS!

Could the spore cells be from outer space? Some scientists claim the spore cells can reproduce at temperatures higher than anything on Earth!

RED RAIN UNDER
A MICROSCOPE

RED RAIN SAMPLE

OTHER THEORIES ABOUT THE RED RAIN IN INDIA, SUCH AS THAT IT WAS CAUSED BY POLLUTION, HAVE BEEN FOUND TO BE UNTRUE.

QUESTIONING THE RED RAIN

There are still many questions about the red rain. If the red particles are spores, why were so many released and carried into the atmosphere at once? Why doesn't this happen more often? Further, more people reported seeing a flash in the sky and hearing a boom before the red rain began, though there was no thunderstorm. That makes some think a meteor passed overhead. Could it have something to do with the red particles? More study is needed to figure it out.

ST. ELMO'S FIRE

It looks like a fire, but doesn't burn. That sounds like a riddle, doesn't it? That's one way to describe the weird weather phenomenon called St. Elmo's Fire. It's not fire, and it's not lightning. It's plasma. Plasma is an ionized gas, which means electrons have been freed from the molecules that make up the gas.

We've already learned that storms create areas of opposite electrical charges, which is why lightning occurs. If the stormy atmosphere is electrically charged enough, electrons—which are negatively charged—free themselves from gas molecules, trying to separate from positively charged **protons**. This tearing apart creates the glow of St. Elmo's Fire. It happens most often on pointed objects, such as a ship's mast, a church steeple, or an airplane wingtip. It may make a crackling or hissing noise.

FREAKY FACTS!

St. Elmo's Fire glows blue because the atmospheric gases nitrogen and oxygen glow blue when they become plasma. Other gases glow different colors when they become plasma.

LUCKY GLOW

The name "St. Elmo's Fire" comes from St. Erasmus, sometimes called Ermo or Elmo, the saint who was said to help sailors. Many of the earliest records of St. Elmo's Fire came from sailors. They noticed it lighting up the masts of their ships, usually at the end of a thunderstorm. It was considered good luck because it meant they had survived a storm at sea. Explorers Ferdinand Magellan and Christopher Columbus both mention the phenomenon in their writings.

THE YEAR WITHOUT A SUMMER

Can you imagine waiting for warm summer days, but they never come? No doubt people were disappointed—and maybe a bit scared—during the summer of 1816. That year was called the "year without a summer" because the summer months were dark, cold, and stormy, especially in North America and Europe. Snow even fell in some areas! Why did this weird weather happen?

In April 1815, Mount Tambora, a volcano in Indonesia, erupted violently. Many think it was the biggest volcanic eruption in recorded history. The eruption killed over 10,000 people. Particles and gases from the eruption flew into the atmosphere over a period of 4 months. They blocked so much sunlight that Earth's average temperature lowered by about 5.4°F (3°C).

FREAKY FACTS!

A resident of Virginia recalled of the summer of 1816: "In June . . . another snowfall came and folk went sleighing [sledding]. On July 4, water froze . . . and snow fell again."

AFTEREFFECTS

Tens of thousands of people died of starvation and disease in Indonesia because of the crop failure caused by the eruption of Mount Tambora. The change in weather affected crops around the world for months after that. Excessive rains caused floods. Cold snaps killed plants and animals. Food became scarce and expensive in many places. Many farmers in New England gave up their land and moved, wanting to start over in another part of the United States.

MOUNT TAMBORA IS STILL CONSIDERED
TO BE AN ACTIVE VOLCANO.

RECORD BREAKERS

In some places, the weather seems weird, but the people there are used to it. Puerto Lopez, Colombia, gets about 500 inches (1,270 cm) of rain each year. Meanwhile, parts of another South American location—the Atacama Desert—haven't seen rain since people began keeping records! Other areas regularly experience extreme heat and extreme cold. Eastern Antarctica holds the frosty record of –135.8°F (–93.2°C), and Death Valley, California, claims the hottest recorded temperature of 134°F (57°C). Amazingly, people and wildlife find ways to live in such extreme climates.

It's important to learn about all kinds of weather: pleasant, nasty, freaky, or even dangerous. Whether you want to know how to dress each day or if you should find shelter for protection, weather is need-to-know information! Is the weather where you live weird?

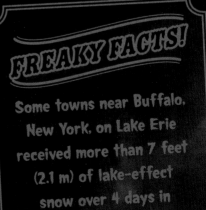

FREAKY FACTS!

Some towns near Buffalo, New York, on Lake Erie received more than 7 feet (2.1 m) of lake-effect snow over 4 days in November 2014.

MORE FREAKY WEATHER EVENTS

UPSIDE-DOWN RAINBOW
LIGHT HITS THE TOP OF
ICE CRYSTALS IN CLOUDS

SNOW ROLLER
PIECE OF SNOW BLOWN
AND ROLLED BY WIND

AURORA
ATMOSPHERIC GASES
AND CHARGED PARTICLES
CREATE LIGHT

MAMMATUS CLOUDS
POUCHES OF CLOUDS
THAT HANG DOWN

RED SPRITE
RED FLASH OF LIGHT
THAT APPEARS ABOVE
A THUNDERSTORM

MICROBURST
COLUMN OF FAST-MOVING,
SINKING AIR

WEATHER-AFFECTING FEATURES

Landforms and water features can make a big impact on weather
and climate. For example, mountain ranges can block rain or keep
it falling on a place. Ocean currents can warm or cool regions,
too. Even large lakes can have an effect on areas. For example,
lake-effect snow is created when air over warm lake waters
rises and condenses into clouds. As the clouds become heavy with
precipitation, more than 5 inches (13 cm) of snow an hour can fall.

GLOSSARY

condense: to change from a gas into a liquid

diameter: the distance from one side of a round object to another through its center

ember: a glowing piece from a fire

hemisphere: one half of Earth

horizontal: level with the line that seems to form where Earth meets the sky

humidity: the amount of moisture in the air

lichen: any of numerous plantlike organisms made up of an alga and a fungus

meteorologist: someone who studies weather, climate, and the atmosphere

phenomenon: facts or events that are observed. The plural form is "phenomena."

plume: something such as smoke, steam, or water that rises into the air in a tall, thin shape

precipitation: rain, snow, sleet, or hail

proton: a very small bit of matter that is part of the nucleus of an atom and has a positive charge

spore: a cell made by some plants that is like a seed and can produce a new plant

FOR MORE INFORMATION

BOOKS

Bredeson, Carmen. *Weird But True Weather*. Berkeley Heights, NJ: Enslow Elementary, 2012.

Furgang, Kathy, with Tim Samaras. *Everything Weather*. Washington, DC: National Geographic, 2012.

Seuling, Barbara. *It Never Rains in Antarctica: And Other Freaky Facts About Climate, Land, and Nature*. Minneapolis, MN: Picture Window Books, 2009.

WEBSITES

How Do Tornadoes Form?
eo.ucar.edu/kids/dangerwx/tornado3.htm
Learn the science behind the formation of tornadoes and learn tornado safety.

Ten Freaky Forces of Nature
kids.nationalgeographic.com/content/kids/en_US/explore/ science/ten-freaky-forces-of-nature/
Read about 10 weird weather phenomena on the National Geographic site.

INDEX